æ perfectiſſimæ religionis augmē

d omnia pietatis ſtudia accendaur.

The Book of the Rose

The Book of the Rose

 è❧

Laura Cerwinske

Designed by J.-C. Suarès

Thames and Hudson

è❧

The Book of the Rose was produced by
Laura Cerwinske Editorial Production
New York, New York

Library of Congress Catalog Card Number:
92–80127

Picture Editor: Peter C. Jones

Graphic Production: Gates Sisters Studio

Printed in Singapore

Dedication

*For Maharaji, who loves roses and who has showered
me with the love and beauty they symbolize. And for
Richard Protovin, for all the love and laughter and
for always seeing me home safely.*

PAGE 2
Lady Lilith, *watercolor by Dante Gabriel Rossetti (detail), 1867.*
PAGE 6
November Roses *by Josef Breitenbach (detail; full image appears on page 160), 1936.
(Houk Friedman Gallery, New York)*

Contents

৯৬

Introduction

The History of an Obsession

છે

When Venus, the Roman goddess of love, was born in the foaming seas near the island of Cyprus, the earth, eager to show that it could equal the gods in the creation of beauty, fashioned a flower unparalleled in its exquisite combination of delicacy and fragrance. The rose, an enduring and universal symbol of passion, devotion, and secrecy, was worshiped by the Greeks, Romans, Persians, Chinese, and Arabians. Aphrodite, the Greek goddess of love, chose it as her personal emblem, as did Dionysus, the Greek god of revelry. Cleopatra is said to have soaked the sails of her ship with rose water so that as she departed from Antony, "the very winds were lovesick." Confucius was inspired by the roses growing in China's Imperial Gardens, and the Phoenicians, who revered the flower, brought rose bushes with them on their travels. In the fifth century B.C., 102 different images of roses appeared on the coins of Rhodes, whose citizens had made it the symbol of their city.

The earliest written mention of the rose appears on Sumerian tablets inscribed some 5,000 years ago. A Sumerian sculpture of the same period depicts a golden ram caught in a thorn bush on which blooms a rose. In the *Iliad* Homer describes the shield used by Achilles in the siege of Troy as decorated with roses and

OPPOSITE
*A 19th-century wallcovering evokes the beauty of a Pompeian mural on the wall of a
Roman catacomb where early Christians painted the flower to symbolize their faith.*
OVERLEAF
Roses in vases and in fabric patterns abound in a library designed by Richard Ridge.
(Peter Vitale)

recounts that Aphrodite came by night to anoint the slain Hector's body with rose oil before it was embalmed. In his epic, Homer introduced the well-known image of "the rosy-fingered dawn." Seven hundred years later, Herodotus, the first historian, visited the gardens of Midas, the exiled King of the Phrygians, and wrote that Midas had brought with him into Macedonia roses with sixty petals. (They are thought to have been the double form of either *Rosa gallica* or of the autumn damask rose.) In the fourth century B.C., Theophrastus, the father of botany, inherited Aristotle's library and wrote a study of the plant world in which he described how the citizens of Philippi, the city founded by Philip II of Macedon, collected wild mountain roses for their gardens. In the Old Testament, the rose is evoked in the Song of Solomon which reads, "I am the Rose of Sharon and the Lily of the Valley." In 1700 B.C. the flower was painted in a fresco in the palace of a Minoan king at Knossos.

The Romans were probably the most lavish celebrants of the rose. On feast days they scattered rose blossoms throughout their streets. Heliogabalus, a wealthy citizen who strewed rose petals over the couches, porticoes, and grounds of his palace, scented the air with fountains of rose water when entertaining. The Emperor Nero showered rose petals on his guests from the ceiling of a dining hall where they had been received on a carpet of rose petals. Nero once insisted that a considerable part of the

ABOVE
"A Discourse on the Virtues of the Rose," from Rosa Gallica *by Champier, 1514.*
OPPOSITE
The Deposition, *by a follower of Rogier van der Weyden (detail), c. 1500. In taking up the symbol of the rose, the Virgin Mary picked up the stem dropped by the goddesses of power, passion, and the blood mysteries of life who had gone before her.*

12

with roses at a service called Dies Rosationis. Hedonistic Romans would literally sleep on "a bed of roses." The proconsul Verres toured Sicily in a sedan chair cushioned with rose-petal pillows.

When the rose was out of season in Italy, the avid Romans, unable to endure an absence of the flower, imported them from North Africa and purchased rose scents from Arab and Indian perfume merchants. Ultimately, the love of the rose inspired a whole society of superior rose gardeners: the pre-Christian Romans of Paestum (just south of Rome) turned the cultivation of the flower into an entrepreneurial endeavor, supplying both the private gardens of nobles and the public rose gardens planted for the pleasure of the citizenry. The poet and satirist Horace once complained that too many roses were grown in Italy and not enough corn. Extracts of the flower were used in candies, wines, puddings, and, of course, in rose water which was added to the bath. Not content with merely practical applications, the Romans also indulged the rose's symbolic use: secret societies often hung a bouquet of roses over the door of a house where a clandestine meeting was being held, hence, sub rosa. A white rose placed over

seashore near Naples be strewn with rose petals in preparation for his visit. Roman heroes were glorified with crowns and garlands of roses. The grave sites of soldiers who fell in battle were decorated

ABOVE AND OPPOSITE
Folio and detail from Mira Calligraphaie Monumenta, *a 16th-century model book of calligraphy, illuminated in pen and ink, watercolors, and gold and silver paint on vellum and paper by Georg Hoefnagel and inscribed by Georg Bocskay.*

a dining room door warned guests not to repeat anything discussed at table. The mystical mythical Roman god of silence, Harpocrates, was said to have been given a rose by Cupid as a bribe so that he would not betray the amours of Venus. Harpocrates was thereafter depicted with a finger of one hand to his lips, a white rose in the other.

With the rise of Christianity, the rose, so closely associated with the passions and imagery of pagan Rome, fell out of favor, and its cultivation nearly vanished throughout Europe. It was grown during the Dark Ages almost exclusively by monks, who used it strictly for medicinal purposes. The

Venerable Bede, the seventh-century monk of Jarrow, was among the few who possessed a copy of Pliny the Elder's 160-volume Historia naturalis of 77 A.D. in which a full chapter is devoted to roses. A ninth-century Swiss monastery included beds of roses in its infirmary garden, and in the thirteenth century, an Augustine abbot (the foster brother of Richard the Lion-hearted) extolled roses as "clad becomingly in ruby purple, blossoming as the glory of the garden."

During the medieval era, the rose emerged within the heart of the mass—in the form of rosary beads made from the fragrant paste of crushed rose petals. A kind of tangible prayer wheel, the rosary is meant to bring about a detachment of the mind, each bead prompting a silent, mantric recitation. Originally the rosary was dedicated to the Lady of the Rose Garden, an image inspired by portrayals of the Virgin Mary which show her surrounded by garlands of roses or in a rose garden.

In twelfth-century France, as the rosary commanded the worshiper's corporal senses, the rose window, a simple circle derived from the occulus of Romanesque cathedrals, grew into a Gothic, flower-

ABOVE
Detail from frontispiece to "Song of the Rose" from the Heldenbuch, *c. 1500*
OPPOSITE AND OVERLEAF
Details from Turkish manuscripts illuminated with roses.

رَبِّ يَسِّرْ وَلَا تَعْسِرْ رَبِّ تَمِّمْ بِالْخَيْرِ آمِينْ

ج	ث	ت	ب	ا
ح	خ	د	ذ	ر
ز	س	ش	ص	ض
ط	ظ	ع	غ	ف

The rose also began to reappear in secular private gardens. Soldiers returning from the Crusades of the twelfth and thirteenth centuries brought back not only descriptions of luxurious Middle Eastern rose gardens, but actual plants as well. In 1453, academicians fleeing to the West from Constantinople (formerly Byzantium) after its capture by the Turks brought with them classical Greek and Latin texts that revealed a knowledge of rose growing far more extensive than anything compiled in the millennium that followed. Contacts between Europe and the newly established Ottoman Empire also opened the eyes of the West to the horticultural practices used so successfully in the gardens of Asia Minor and Persia. Among the many unfamiliar plants that grew there were two varieties of yellow roses.

like form and drew attention heavenward. With the development of stained glass, the simple circle had gained geometrical intricacy and mystical power: a cathedral flooded with jewel-colored light (thought to possess healing powers), refracted from floor to ceiling and emanating from a mandala of divine symbols, could mesmerize a worshiper. Suspended between floor and vault—as if between heaven and earth—the rose window radiated like a heavenly sphere, a beautifully cut gemstone, drawing the worshiper into its energy, and in turn, focusing the light of the soul into the ultimate temple of the spirit.

The asceticism of the medieval era eventually gave way to the acceptance of beauty for its own sake, and the flower regained its prominence in art, poetry, heraldry, and legend. One example of a legend is "The White Rose of the Orient," the story of a Christian knight named Henry who during the Crusades visited the Gardens of Solomon in Damascus. Under the cypresses, Henry watched

ABOVE
Roses, *albumen print by Charles Aubry, 1860-69.*
OPPOSITE
Detail of "Rosa alba foliacea" from Les Roses *by Pierre Joseph Redouté, 1817-1824.*
(W. Graham Arader III Gallery, New York)

the rose-pickers—Saracen women who carried on their heads huge baskets of red, pink, and white petals for making attar of roses. Among these women was a Persian slave girl named Sheramur who sang a sweetly compelling song as she plucked. Intoxicated as much by her melody as by the perfumed air, Henry pleaded with her to sing for him alone.

That evening, Sheramur sat at his feet and sang in her purest voice. Overcome with the beauty of the slave girl and her melody, Henry begged to know the meaning of the song. "It is the legend of the birth of the red rose," she whispered. "It tells how, when the first white rose bloomed, the nightingale was seized with such love for the flower that he flung himself against it and was pierced by its thorns. As he lay upon its petals dying, his blood colored the white bosom of the rose a dark crimson, and so it has bloomed ever since." Observing the delicate face and pallid ivory skin of Sheramur, Sir Henry began to think of her, too, as a white rose. He wondered whether the love-sacrifice of a bleeding heart would turn her into a crimson rose—a strange thought for a Christian knight to entertain about a Saracen woman. For in the end, it was he who would die of a captive heart and Sheramur who would escape into the arms of a princely lover.

❧

In the sixteenth century, the English herbalist John Gerard composed the most useful and readable treatise published to date for those interested in the cultivation of roses. His *Herball*—which ultimately grew to 1,600 pages of text on 2,850 plants with woodcut illustrations—described fourteen different roses. In 1629, a London apothecary named John Parkinson, in a work called *Paradisi,* reported the existence of twenty-four varieties. Linnaeus's 1753 *Species plantarum,* a landmark in botanical history, included twelve species of roses. Philip Miller's *Gardener's Dictionary* adopted the Linnaean system and named twenty-six. A nursery catalogue of the same era listed forty-four.

While scientists of the eighteenth century broadened awareness of the rose in the horticultural world, two women of the French court revived its romantic mystique. The Marquise de Pompadour, the official mistress of Louis XV, seldom made a public appearance without a rose bouquet at her

OPPOSITE
Detail of "Rosa rapa" from Les Roses *by Pierre Joseph Redouté, 1817-1824.*
(W. Graham Arader III Gallery, New York)

bosom or a garland lining the hem of her gown. Her successor, Madame du Barry, slept under a canopy "whose long sweeping silk curtains were embroidered with patterns of cascading roses."

It was not until the nineteenth century, however, that an empress whose middle name was Rose finally elevated the flower's stature from a medicinal and ornamental blossom to a fashionable plant cultivated in the highest circles of French horticulture. Josephine, the wife of Napoleon I, had developed a love for roses during her childhood on the island of Martinique. She brought about a "rose renaissance" when she determined to grow every known variety of the flower at Malmaison, her country house. Its rooms were decorated with botanical "trees" on whose wrought-iron branches were hung crystal

"Dr. and Mrs. Sill in Carriage," c. 1895.

24

vials displaying the most perfect specimens from each bush in bloom.

Although Josephine imported plants from all over the world, she favored English roses along with the naturalistic English landscape style, a seemingly disordered but carefully planned profusion of different species and varieties. With its sweeping lawns interspersed with glades and waterfalls, its geometri- cally shaped flower beds and winding grass paths that led to a rose-covered pergola, Josephine's garden was one of the first in Europe to include a section devoted exclusively to roses. She commissioned André Dupont, who had worked with roses on the grounds of the Luxembourg palace and was an enthusiastic hybridizer, to assemble a magnificent collection. To put the finest knowledge and rose

Prima ballerina Patricia McBride is showered with roses as she takes the final curtain call of her career with the New York City Ballet. (Paul Kolnik)

eties over succeeding years. Although the garden did not survive Josephine's death, her roses were immortalized by artist Pierre-Joseph Redouté, whom she had commissioned to catalogue the collection. This compilation of incomparable watercolor renderings, entitled *Les Roses,* was first printed in 1817 and is still regarded as one of the world's greatest works of botanical illustration.

Josephine's roses included 167 types of Gallicas, twenty-seven Centifolias, three Mosses, twenty-two Chinas, nine Damasks, four Spinosissimas, eight Albas, three Foetidas, and nine Musks—a fair representation of the roses popular in Europe at the beginning of the nineteenth century. The Gallica, also known as the French Rose, is considered the oldest variety. It was cultivated as early as the twelfth century B.C. by the Persians, who used it as, among other purposes, a religious symbol. It was known to have flourished later throughout the entire Mediterranean. The Gallicas and Centifolias, which bloom once a year—in May or June—were among the first roses brought to the West from the Near East and are part of a group referred to as "old fashioned." The Damasks, originally grown by the Romans, were

plants at her disposal, she even arranged to have John Kennedy of Hammersmith, a highly regarded London nursery, travel freely between England and France in the midst of the two countries' hostilities—even as Napoleon was ordering his troops to confiscate any horticultural specimens found on British ships. Other roses for the garden came from Jacques-Martin Cels, the Cultivateur de l'Institut National de France, as well as from the country's best nurseries.

Between 1798, when she began her efforts, and 1814, when she died, Josephine collected more than 250 rose plants. Her endeavor provided the impetus to French rose breeders to produce many new vari-

ABOVE
The romance of the rose as illustrated in early-20th-century postcards.
(Lisa S. Adelson Collection)
OPPOSITE
A photograph taken for an advertisement for Tea Rose perfume. (John Chan)

prized for their ability to bloom twice a year and for their heady fragrance. The Chinas or China Teas, newer varieties, were introduced to European and American gardens in the early 1800s, their names derived from their place of origin and from the fact that they arrived on tea traders' ships and had a scent reminiscent of fresh tea leaves. They had been discovered in 1789 in a botanical garden in Calcutta by a British sea captain where they had been brought from China by the East India Company. Because they had large blossoms and flowered continuously, they became, despite their fragility, an instant rage in Europe. Eventually, they were crossed with other varieties of roses in an effort to hybridize a flower that would combine hardiness with continuous bloom. Josephine's China Roses were ultimately hybridized into generations of flowers that display all manner of color, size, and character.

&

The written history of the rose in North America begins with Christopher Columbus. The day before sighting the shores of the New World, he had, according to his ship's log, pulled a rose bush from the ocean, where it was floating in the waters beside his becalmed vessel. The rescue of the rose, the explorer reported, renewed his spirits.

Even before Columbus, it is known that the Indians of the James River Valley planted wild roses to beautify their camps, making the flower one of the first to be cultivated for its ornamental quality. The pilgrims who settled the Plymouth Colony in 1620 planted "an abundance of roses, white, red, and damask, single but very sweete indeed."

When William Penn visited Europe in the late seventeenth century, he was inspired by the roses he found in both public and private gardens. Upon his return to America, he brought eighteen rose bushes with him and elaborated upon their beauty and medicinal value in his *Book of Physics*. He advised, for example, that if an ailment is "not exactly romantic, comfort ye brains…with a handful of rose blossoms, cloves, mace, nutmeg, all in a powder." Penn's family is also known to have been ardent about the flower; they rented parcels of their land for the payment each year of one red rose.

Presidents Washington and Jefferson, both devout gardeners, made the cultivation of roses a

OPPOSITE
Detail of "Grand Dessin de Large," French block print in a sample book of hand-blocked wallcoverings designed by Jules Desfosse for the Exposition Universale of 1855.
(Leslie Jean-Bart)

significant activity on their estates. Mount Vernon had so many rose bushes that, on some occasions, picking all the blossoms required two whole days. At Monticello, however, rose bushes were regarded more as shrubs for hedging and for soil stabilization than as adornments to the flowerbed.

Traditionally, roses have been given romantic names. The Greeks based theirs on mythological deities, such as Bouquet of Venus, Temple of Apollo, and Beautiful Juno. The French under Napoleon used the names of court favorites—Grand Napoleon coming at the head of their registry, followed by a list of mesdames, marquis, dukes, and duchesses, such as the Duke and Duchess of Bedford. In England, roses were named for royalty and titled persons, such as Queen Victoria, The Duke of Wellington, and Lady Hillington. The Chinese chose more poetic and metaphysical names, such as Tiny Jade Shoulders, Three Rays of Dawn, Seven Precious Petals, and Precious-Scented Ivory.

As opposed to the tight, high-centered blossom of "Modern" roses, those of "Old" roses—flowers that appeared before the introduction of the first Hybrid Tea rose, "La France," in 1867—may be flattened like architectural rosettes, overblown like a petticoat, or cupped with the petals wrapped tightly around the center. The colors of "Old" roses are subtler and softer than the "Moderns," and their scents are stronger and more varied (they range from spicy—myrrh, cinnamon, and clove—to fruity—apple, mango, orange, pineapple, and banana).

As an embodiment of the divine, the rose has figured in virtually every mystical tradition. In her *Book of Spiritual Grace,* Saint Matilda describes the three perfumes that symbolize divine love, the first in sweetness and desirability being rose water. Rose incense was found on the altars of Zoroastrians and Confucians as well as in the temples of Memphis and Jerusalem where lamp oils and wax tapers were scented. The Brahmin image of paradise centers around a silver rose. Mohammed is said to have given birth to the white rose during his ascent to heaven. Lakshmi, the Indian keeper of fortune and wealth, slept in a thousand-petaled rose. And the Peruvian Eve plucked not an apple, but a rose from the Garden of Eden.

OPPOSITE

Tilla Durieux, *by Pierre Auguste Renoir (detail), 1914. The artist is known to have associated the rose with physical allure. Its representation in this painting connotes his high estimation of Miss Durieux's beauty.*

Decorative Roses

❧

Thirty thousand guests of all classes gathered at the Winter Palace in Saint Petersburg for the annual New Year's open house. Knowing that the ladies of nobility would be attired in magnificent brocades, satins, and jewels, Catherine the Great decided to titillate the assembly by dressing in a starkly simple costume. Unlike her coronation gown of silver brocade embroidered with gold threads and covered with a mantle made from four thousand ermine pelts, and her pearl- and jewel-embellished finery reserved for affairs of state, the white silk dress she chose for this evening was worn over a small hoop and decorated with only a ruby and diamond brooch at the bodice. In her hair, tied in a "foxtail" at the back of her head, she wore a single gold rose, its stem and thorns burnished, its bud and leaves set with rubies and emeralds. The Empress's daring effect was as dramatic as if she had appeared in full imperial regalia, and it heightened the already vast intrigue that surrounded her love life. Did the rose suggest she was in the first blush of excitement over a new consort? Or that, with her own eye, she was surveying the gathering for romantic prospects?

Beginning in the fifteenth century, when Botticelli's Venus ascended from the sea in a shower of rose petals, the flower's ties to the Virgin diminished and its association with the goddess of love again blossomed. By the eighteenth century, the rose, no longer simply a symbol of spiritual purity, had come to be regarded as an object of beauty in itself, an expression of romance and passion.

OPPOSITE
Detail of Fragonard's The Lover Crowned, *c. 1771. A quintessential example of rococo painting, it illustrates the period's—as well as Madame du Barry's—predilection for the rose. (The Frick Collection, New York)*

The rose's romantic associations flourished in the fashions of eighteenth-century France when aristocratic dress was, as the fashion writer André Leon Talley described it, "laden with the florascape; women often carried extremes to the limit when they promenaded in the parks…and used long garlands of fresh roses as a flirtatious device second only to a fan inlaid with roses in pearl or diamante."

In the many portraits painted of Madame de Pompadour, she is almost never without a rose. Like the Empress of Russia, she well understood how to apply her intelligence and keen eye to the cultural life of the court. As an untitled consort, however, her role was to amuse, entertain, and assist the man she loved. In this capacity she looked to roses to heighten both her personal beauty and the beauty she cultivated in her surroundings. Her portrait by Boucher shows her dressed in a voluminous gown embroidered from hem to shoulders with clusters of roses, with tiny roses pinned in her hair and two roses lying at her feet. Two hundred years later, the English writer Sacheverell Sitwell described the Belle de Crecy, a rose that was grown in Pompadour's garden, as having a scent that "takes you in a breath into the eighteenth century, while {its} rose pink petals and jade green leaves make one think of the bows and ribbons of Pompadour by Boucher."

Madame de Pompadour's successor, Madame du Barry, possessed an even greater passion for roses. Diamonds in the shapes of roses sparkled on her skirts. In a painting by François Drouais she is seen as the goddess Flora, with a wreath of pink roses in her hair and a garland of the same sweet blooms in her hands. She gave her name to the color "Rose du Barry," and like Pompadour was fond of appearing in public in rose-embellished gowns. To one court wedding, for example, she wore a silver dress embroidered with green and rose-colored butterflies and the neckline embroidered with tiny roses.

A century later, the artist F. X. Winterhalter painted the French Empress Eugénie in a lavishly crinolined dress decorated with roses. With coquettish symbolism, the extravagant circumference of the crinoline warns a suitor to keep his distance, while the roses beckon him. A garden scene painted by Monet a few years later shows ladies protected by their crinolines from the thorny rose bushes past which they stroll.

The dress style of the late nineteenth century

called for rose decoration at the breast and the waist, a fashion that did not change with the naughty nineties, except for the addition of silk, tulle, or other fabric to the dress at the bottom and the thighs. By the turn of the century, when Aubrey Beardsley took up the depiction of the rose—on the gown of his handsome flagellant, at the feet of the transsexual Pierrot, beside his barefoot Salome, and in the hand of his voluptuous *Lady with the Rose*—it had gained distinct eroticism.

In the original production of Fokine's ballet *Le Spectre de la Rose*, inspired by the poem by Théophile Gautier, Nijinsky played the Spirit of the Rose, a gauzy mysterious figure, not man, not rose, but the essence of each. His costume, a close-fitting silk elastic sweater, covered nearly all his body and was blanketed with roses in pink, lavender, and red. The costume's designer, Léon Bakst, took great pains to ensure that each rose petal was cut differently and that some of the petals would appear half faded and others fresh. Before a performance, each petal was curled with hot tongs.

Like Bakst, the revolutionary early-twentieth-century couturier Paul Poiret was also often asked to do costumes for the stage. Many stars, such as the Ballets Russes dancer Ida Rubinstein, loved his designs and delighted in parading her "Poiret fantasies" through the middle of the streets of Paris, bringing traffic to a screeching halt. Unlike Rubinstein, the dance hall performer Mistinguett wore Poiret's creations only at the insistence of her manager. For a number at the Casino de Paris in which she was to represent a rose, Poiret designed a costume made of a hoop skirt covered with immense petals from which grew a green velvet corselet representing a leaf of the flower. The headpiece consisted of a stalk of long green velvet branches covered with diamonds. When presented with the costume, Mistinguett cried, "I can't dance in that!" To which Poiret retorted, "You can't dance in anything!"

Poiret was the first of the fashion celebrities. His one-piece straight-falling gowns, pantaloons, fitted tubes with slit skirts, kimono-like jackets, long tunics and saris liberated women from the cruelly binding corset. He made his new sleek, reedy silhouette even more startling by using a brilliant color palette full of reds and vermilions, royal blues, yellows, and greens. Among the most notable of his embellishments was a highly stylized rosebud design, so closely associated

with his signature that it became known as the Poiret rose. Abstracted with geometric precision into a highly modern, yet almost Oriental-looking motif, it was applied to any number of his dresses and accessories.

According to the couturier Valentino, roses impose a "tranquility of peace upon the image of woman. Dresses with oversized roses...are something bold and yet mysterious, an evocative symbol of life, the earth, civilization and the beauty of creation." In 1959, in the first of his own collections, Valentino used "an escapade rose, a rose full of light in the gradient mauve to ivory petals as a bunch on the hem of a cloqué black strapless cocktail dress." Later, he took an Edwardian evening shirt "with sleeves worked like birdcages in guipure lace and then slipped bouquets of silk cabbage roses between the outer surface and the lining for a woman to enjoy privately." André Leon Talley has described how Valentino once "clipped for an evening pouf, a pale rose of silk organza petals to glide over his double black ballooning short dance skirt. Roses sprouted inside grained gazar silk ruffles, and as embroidery...worked in silk...on the shoulders of his breezeaway night toppers. {He used} one giant rose as the focus on the décolleté of a chiffon tea dress…and a universal rose…in a soft eighteenth-century blurred print on mousseline de soie."

Luxurious and voluptuous, the rose appears in the fashions of other contemporary designers such as Oscar de la Renta and Emanuel Ungaro. Attracted to the flower's uplifting appeal, they apply it in silk and in satin, in beads and in printed pattern, and on all manner of accessories from shoes, handbags, and hats to colorful decorative ornaments.

ઝ

The rose has appeared in jewelry since monarchs and popes first commissioned representations of the flower in gemstones and precious metals. From the early Renaissance, it was customary for the Pope to bless a gold rose and send it to a sovereign of a Roman Catholic state as a token of esteem. Gold, precious and immutable, alluded to the immortality of the soul; the flower symbolized the frailty of the body and the shortness of life. The same message always accompanied the papal gift: "Accept this rose at our hand who, albeit unworthy, holds the place of God on earth, by which rose is typified the joy of the

Oscar de la Renta's pink rosebud of a wedding gown is a confection of satin and tulle.

heavenly Jerusalem and of the Church Militant by which to all the faithful in Christ is manifested that most beauteous flower, which is the joy and crown of all saints. Receive, then, thou dearly beloved son, who art, according to the age, noble, potent, and endowed with many virtues, that thou mayest be more fully ennobled with every virtue in Christ our Lord, as a rose planted by the streams of many waters."

One papal gold rose was sent to the devout Empress Eugénie. It became one of her most treasured possessions, and, after the fall of the Second Empire, she mourned its loss more than almost any other of her possessions. Years later, an anonymous package was delivered to her home in exile. It contained the gold rose, salvaged somehow from the ruins of the Tuileries. The Empress is said to have kept it by her side until her death nearly fifty years later.

Gold roses were also found in the treasuries of the Incas of Peru, who skillfully imitated in gold all the flowers that flourished in their land. When the Inca king was captured by the Spanish conquistador Pizarro, the ruler offered to ransom his own life with enough gold to fill a room twenty-two feet long and seventeen feet wide. Natives from the far-thest parts of Peru offered up their gold objects, including gold roses, to save their monarch. But the conquistador killed the king and melted down the priceless treasure of gold objects and shipped them as ingots to Spain.

Outside of papal and monarchal circles, the rose has enjoyed a long history of literal and inventive replication by jewelers and other artists. In the six-teenth century, Benvenuto Cellini fashioned roses in enamel, gold, and pearls. A suitor of Queen Elizabeth I, the Duc d'Alençon, tried to win her royal heart with gifts of splendid jewels, among them a rose in white enamel. One of the Queen's most elaborate presents on New Year's Day of 1571 was a white rose of York surrounded by the red roses of Lancaster in rubies and enamel. Two centuries later diamond ornaments in the form of rose wreaths and garlands became fashionable. Some were made with hidden springs that caused the jeweled flowers to nod and shimmer as the wearer moved.

To relieve the boredom of the Russian aristocra-cy during their long, bitter gray winters, the famed jeweler to the czars, Peter Carl Fabergé, crafted flowers for his clients out of a broad and exotic

PRECEDING PAGES
Silk Roses *by George Tscherny, 1990.*

44

palette of hardstone, precious metals, and enamels. By maintaining a hothouse at the top of his Moscow shop, he was able to study and copy blossoms year round. In the middle of a freezing February he might devise, for example, a small bouquet of yellow enamel roses with a rose-diamond center and leaves carved of nephrite. The flowers' gold stems would be arranged in a crystal vase, also of his design. When placed on the writing desk of the wife of a Saint Petersburg noble, the jeweled roses brought a vernal radiance to her dim salon.

Fabergé realized his flowers with poetry and precision. His eye was absolute, and while he might affect a tone of humor in his classically carved rhodonite pig, or jasper monkey, or gold and agate kiwi, he was reverent in his approach to flowers. H.C. Bainbridge, who wrote on Fabergé's life, saw in the master a piety in his floral representations: "However you may play tricks with animals, you cannot be funny with flowers. They are the perfection of all created things. Absolute aristocrats, you cannot subordinate them. They will do nothing for you except in their own sweet way …and if you would represent them, you must do so petal for petal, pistil by pistil, and leaf for leaf."

Brenda Boozer as Octavian, a male role written for a mezzo, presents a silver rose to his beloved Sophie in a New York Metropolitan Opera production of Strauss's Der Rosenkavalier. *(Winne Klotz)*

In a more dramatic incarnation, a silver rose is the star of *Der Rosenkavalier,* the twentieth-century Richard Strauss opera. In the second act, the hero, Octavian, approaches the heroine, Sophie, rose in hand. Though he attempts to project an air of importance, he blushes with anticipation. Moved by his handsome shyness, Sophie grows pale. "I have the honor, in the name of my cousin, to present the rose of love to his bride," he announces. "I am grateful to my lord," she replies, pressing her nose to the flower. "It has a strong scent, like a real rose." He tells her that it is perfumed with Persian attar, and she answers, "It is like a rose from Paradise, do you not agree?" Octavian bows over the flower, the incarnation of their destiny, and then looks up at Sophie. "It is like a greeting from Heaven…unbearably sweet."

Compelled by his experience of the *Spectre de la Rose,* Paul Iribe, the great Art Nouveau designer and a colleague of Paul Poiret, used a golden rose as a personal symbol in his fashion, theater, and advertising work and in eleven jewelry designs executed at the suggestion of the artist José Maria Sert. The Iribe rose inspired carpet designs and textiles, was used in advertisements for the perfume manufacturer Lubin, and appeared in jewelry by LaCloche and Boucheron.

Before the house of Cartier offered dimensional representations of roses in its jewelry, it favored the stylized forms of Art Deco and, earlier, neo-Etruscan and neo-Roman fashions. In 1947, an Etruscan-style rose-blossom tiara from Cartier's in London, with individual blooms that could be detached and worn separately as brooches, was presented to the Princess Elizabeth.

❧

Even before its elevation to the worlds of fashion and jewelry, the rose drew avid interest as a decorative and heraldic motif. In the East, the rosette with its stylized geometric formations of circles, squares, and octagons first appeared in the weaving of Chinese silk textiles during the Mongol dynasty of the fourteenth century. In the West, the wild rose, easy to draw and clearly recognizable from afar, was an icon of medieval heraldry. Edward I of England, for instance, chose a golden rose to represent the royal family during his reign from 1272 to 1307. In the fifteenth century, Edward IV chose a *rose en soleil*—a white rose framed in a circle of sun rays. Henry IV, the first

OPPOSITE
Glass tesserae form a pattern of roses in the shade of a lamp designed in the late 19th century by Louis Comfort Tiffany.

46

Lancastrian king, selected for his badge a red rose.

In the play *Henry VI, Part I,* Shakespeare dramatized the most famous appropriation of the flower by having the two sides in the War of the Roses choose their emblems during a quarrel in the Temple Garden in London—the House of Lancaster picking a red rose for its coat of arms and the House of York a white. At the end of the war, what came to be known as the Tudor rose, a white rose placed in the center of a red rose, surmounted by a crown, was adopted as a badge of reconciliation. Kings Henry VII and Henry VIII later chose for their heraldic symbols this double rose with its outer ring of red petals and center of white ones. Edward VI favored a Tudor rose impaled on a pomegranate, and Queen Elizabeth, a Tudor rose accompanied by the motto "Rose sine spina," meaning the rose without thorns. The rose with thorns was used by the Stuarts who chose an image of a rose divided into halves. Queen Anne adopted as her personal badge the rose and thistle growing from the same stalk. Eventually, the rose became the national emblem of England (as it also is of Czechoslovakia, Poland, Romania, Honduras, and Iran). When a rose is added to an English coat of arms, it indicates that the wearer is seventh in line of succession to the individual whose coat of arms he is bearing. The seventh son of a seventh son is entitled to wear two roses.

In France, roses were woven into the Unicorn tapestries made for Anne of Brittany in celebration of her marriage to Louis XII of France in 1499 and were among the multitude of flowers represented in the "millefleurs" tapestries produced during the 1500s. Renowned for their naturalism and harmonious combinations of colors—little flowers on pink or blue backgrounds—these French weavings exhibit a deep feeling for nature with their exuberant representations of garden and field.

Throughout the Gothic era, a highly stylized representation of the rose was used in both ecclesiastical and secular art. The Italians preferred the trefoil or quatrefoil rose in both carved and painted ornament, while the English selected the cinquefoil. By the late seventeenth century, the rose had become a favored design for tole ware, the highly decorated japanned (lacquered) metalware developed in England during that time. To manufacture tole, thin metal plates were molded into useful and ornamental household utensils such as trays, tea and coffee pots, vases, and cachepots. Nosegays and delicate swags of roses—the most copied motifs—were hand painted with an enamel made from coal by-products, which when fired became impervious to heat and moisture. Most tole artists had previously worked in porcelain potteries and applied china-painting technique to tole decoration. In France, where tole ware was introduced during the Directoire period, aristocratic households used it to replace their silverware, which had been melted down during the Revolution.

Tole ware and its palette of bright-painted rose designs did not reach America until the nineteenth century when decorative stenciling was in vogue. Inexpensive and simple to apply, it was adopted as a trade by itinerant artists who decorated the walls of private homes in exchange for board and a nominal fee. The two patterns they used most commonly were a border of roses entwined with other garden flowers and repeats of stylized rosettes.

≈

The art of producing decorative porcelain became an obsession in the seventeenth and eighteenth centuries in Europe as well as in Russia. Peter the Great had sent emissaries to Peking to wrest from the Chinese the secrets of their exquisite ware—and failed. During the reign of his daughter, Empress Elizabeth, the first Russian porcelain formulas and technology were created, and the Imperial Porcelain Factory was established. Catherine the Great, with characteristic ambition, furthered the evolving art of porcelain production by importing highly skilled painters, modelers, and craftsmen from Germany, Austria, France, and Scandinavia. In time, foreign entrepreneurs, attracted by the considerable financial opportunities in Russia, followed these artists and began establishing private factories. Most prominent among these was one opened in Moscow in 1766 by Francis Gardner, an English businessman. Catherine was so impressed by the beauty and workmanship of his items that she ordered a number of services, among them the Meissen Rose (later known as the Gardner Rose) dinner service. Each sweet delicate bouquet, painted on a white background, hosts a plump newly blooming red rose. A Sèvres pattern service, made in the Russian Imperial Porcelain Factory during the reign of Alexander III, shows a similar rose in full

OPPOSITE
A soft paste porcelain plate painted by Antoine Capelle and Jacques-François-Louis de la Roche and gilded by Henri Prevost the Younger in 1782.

bloom, as do numerous tea services, cake baskets, and tureens crafted from Catherine's time through the nineteenth century. A *tête-à-tête* (a service consisting of two coffee cups and saucers with a creamer and sugar bowl on a tray) made during the time of Alexander I is decorated with sprigs of roses and garlands of rose leaves; a service ordered by Nicholas I as a present to Mahmud II, the Sultan of Turkey, is painted with sprays of pink roses and trailing gilt scrolls; the dinner and pirozhki plates of the Corbie Service, originally produced in France and added to by the Imperial Porcelain Factory, have roses centered in a frame of overscaled grapes and grape leaves; a coffee service from the Peterhof, the summer palace, sets roses in a multicolored bouquet against a blue, gold, and white ground; Peterhof's banquet service, intended for ceremonial dinners, numbered over 5,500 pieces, each decorated with sprigs and bouquets of roses; and an intricately decorated tureen and stand with four plates in cobalt blue and gilded procelain were designed with a rose pattern based on a Sèvres service given by Louis XV to Christian VII of Denmark.

Among the most richly painted of the Russian

porcelains are the plates decorated in the style of Redouté at the Yousoupoff Factory, owned by the former head of the Imperial Porcelain Factory, Prince Nicholas Borisovich Yousoupoff. All the production of this factory was limited to his personal use. Painted on imported blanks, each plate features one of Redouté's roses from Josephine's garden within a gilt border, with the name of the rose inscribed in French under the design. Gilt inscriptions on the back of some of the plates indicate volume and page number from *Les Roses*.

During the rococo period and the years of rapid change in style that followed, when walls were deco-

rated with a polychromed or woven silk motif, a room's furniture and accessories often echoed the designs. Decorative roses ran riot across windows, floors, tables, chests, and chairs, as well as the porcelains of French, Italian, and German palaces and haute bourgeoise houses. Rose patterns appeared in rugs and tapestries, in draperies and wall sconces, in the hand-painted designs and marquetry inlays of fine furniture, in woven upholstery, and in porcelain urns, vases, and tableware.

To have flowers on the table was *de rigueur*, and whether one used fresh, silk, or porcelain flowers depended on the time of year. The Paris dealer Duperron, who specialized in flowers made of silk and feathers, advertised "toutes sortes de beaux Bouquets pour les Services de Tables." The porcelain maker Vincennes found his first great commercial success in the production of porcelain flowers to be used as table ornaments. Meissen, likewise, crafted ensembles of porcelain vases and baskets with flowers, among them roses mounted on stems with leaves of green-painted metal.

For the artists at Sèvres, flowers were a constant source of inspiration. The rose, traditional among their many patterns, appeared singly, in posies, and bouquets, combined with ribbons, hung as garlands, combined with fruit, and arranged in baskets or vases. One design that proved particularly popular in vases was of individual roses painted in white roundels (occasionally speckled in blue or gold) which were edged with a plain gold band or with gilded laurel leaves. Five mounted vases of this design on a turquoise-blue background were sold to Madame du Barry in 1770.

The precedent of the rose-embellished interior continued to be expanded and modified throughout the nineteenth century as the flower found expression in the decoration of silver, glass, fabric, and

ABOVE
Detail of a Baccarat cut glass vase, c. 1830, with enameled foil medallion with roses.
(Mallett & Son Ltd., London)
OPPOSITE
Willliam Morris's "Rose" is an example of how the artist retained the natural form
of the flower in his stylized designs.

artists of the Vienna Succession movement). Mackintosh believed that flowers gave "that feeling of sunshine and fresh air so desired by the modern mind," and that every artist should strive "to make his flower a beautiful living thing, something that will convince the world that there may be, that there are, things more precious, more beautiful, more lasting than life. But to do this you must offer real living, beautifully colored flowers, flowers that grow not from above, but above the green leaf…real flowers springing from your own soul, not even cut flowers….You must offer the flowers of the art that is in you…flowers that will change a colorless, cheerless life into an animated thoughtful thing." Roses, drawn from life, appear in Mackintosh's sketchbooks and were applied as decorative devices to

wallpaper. Even the Houses of Parliament commissioned a "rose and coronet" wallpaper.

The Arts and Crafts movement of the early twentieth century employed several versions of the rose. The medieval briar rose, depicted on a thorny stem, appears often in rubbed brick panels set into garden walls. Charles Rennie Mackintosh, the leader of the movement's Glasgow School, preferred stylized, tightly budded roses, sometimes called roseballs, which he adopted as his personal symbol (as did a number of

ABOVE LEFT
Tiffany & Co.'s "Rose" brooch of diamonds set in platinum and 18K gold.
ABOVE RIGHT
A double rose brooch in diamonds and rubies from Van Cleef & Arpels.
OPPOSITE
Satin and chiffon roses embellish mules by Susan Bennis Warren Edwards. (Jennifer Krogh)

his furniture, wall hangings, light fixtures, and flower holders. Discreet, formalized, linear roses in a delicate color scheme of white, silver, and pink represented the central motif of his Rose Boudoir, a major exhibit designed for the International Exhibition of Modern and Decorative Art in Turin in 1902.

Throughout the 1920s and 30s, as the influence of the German Bauhaus grew, the cerebral and scientific bent of modernism extended from Europe around the world. The decorative arts, like the fine arts and architecture, reflected, to a degree, modernism's taste for the unornamented and the abstract and its disinterest in the narrative and the pictorial. However, unlike other evocative, symbolic, and romantic images that disappeared from the vocabulary of high design, the rose endured. Despite the quixotic tastes of the twentieth century's style-makers, the rose has continued to bloom in the porcelain and silver patterns of the most fashionably set tables, to flow from the pens of graphic designers, costume designers, scenic designers, and illustrators, and to dazzle on the runways of the haute couture houses.

OPPOSITE
Fashion designer Emanuel Ungaro mixed roses with checks in a chic spring ensemble.
ABOVE
Roses are part of a sultry, sophisticated image by photographer William Klein in Hat and Three Roses, *a silver print, 1956. (Gallerie Zabriskie, Paris)*

Fantin
Juillet 1875

Still Lifes with Roses

☙

His face flushed from the cold, Henri Fantin-Latour pulled tighter the scarf wrapped around his neck. He wore several sweaters under his bulky smock and heavy carpet slippers on his feet. Yet, despite the relentless chill that pervaded his Paris studio, the artist was determined to complete the still life he had begun months earlier at the home of his English friends and patrons, Mr. and Mrs. Edwin Edwards. Fantin had approached this canvas, as he did all others, by painting the background in neutral tones from light to dark and weaving a complex web of marks into and over it. This practice, used by Titian in his portraits, gives the background a subtle richness, filling it with texture and life.

On a table next to his easel, Fantin arranged a bouquet of red, white, and yellow roses in various stages of bloom. At the foot of the vase he lay a pale peach Damask, its leaf and unopened bud poignant in their inertness. Mr. and Mrs. Edwards had suggested to the artist that Fantin use plain tabletops in his flower paintings in order to show to best advantage his great skill in rendering texture and color. He had chosen the colors in this bouquet especially for their luminosity, for the way the light caressed and molded the grain and tissue of each flower, almost as if it were a human face. He was more than a painter of flowers and portraits, Fantin was an artist of light and color.

OPPOSITE
White Roses *by Fantin-Latour, 1875. The artist's voluptuous brushwork matched the lushness of his subject.*
OVERLEAF
Still Life with Scattered Roses *by Lanny Provo, 1990.*

dissatisfied with his endeavor. "Never have I had more ideas about Art, and I am obliged to do flowers," he wrote, wishing instead that he were painting the allegorical compositions he considered a more worthy pursuit. It was true that flower painting provided him a living and that he felt free from his innate reserve only during his quiet communion with these still lifes. But his academic bent made it hard for him to justify the time and study given over to flowers, rather than more serious allegorical subjects. He also retained doubts about the aesthetic sensibilities of the English, who had become the first to enjoy and collect his art, lamenting that, in general, they were easily impressed by sentimental subjects in elaborate frames. Why, one Englishwoman had so missed the point of his work that she asked if he might give her lessons—not in painting but in flower arranging!

Fantin had learned to enliven each petal with a touch of gold or silver and he described with simple direct brush strokes the opulence of the blooms. Yet, as his paintings grew in beauty, he grew more

Nevertheless, his acquaintance with the English had been fruitful. He had first visited Britain with his colleague James McNeill Whistler, whom he had met along with Manet and Berthe Morisot at the Louvre where they were all studying and copying old masters. During that trip he was befriended by the pre-

Political Allegory with Flowers, *albumen print by Charles de Forest Fredricks, c. 1889-94.*

Raphaelites, who introduced him to a number of London art dealers and to the Edwardses. The couple found his work finely observed and full of inner spark and invited him to come paint at their country estate. They bought almost all the flower still lifes he produced there. The English garden designer Gertrude Jekyll, herself a fine painter, would write that Fantin's "genius and sympathy enabled him to show on his canvas not only the {flowers'} intrinsic beauty and dignity, but a pathetic suggestion of their relation to human life and happiness."

Fantin could count a number of the Dutch masters as his predecessors, among them Seghers, the Jesuit from Antwerp who gave his "Nativities" crowns of roses, and van Huysum, who painted the trembling of dew drops and butterfly wings on the leaf of a rosebush. Fantin's work, however, is less analytical and more emotive: it possesses, in addition to his own dazzling brush work, the intimacy of Chardin and the symphony of colors of Delacroix. Marcel Proust described him as an artist who looks "deep inside himself and inside the bouquet of flowers where the delicately scented roses multiply in a thousand other colors, a thousand other perfumes."

Perhaps, as the Edwardses advised, "If one painted still lifes well, one could paint the universe."

&

Fantin-Latour's nineteenth-century flower paintings are indisputably among the most luscious and com-

In a 17th-century still life by Jan van Kessel, the Elder, the roses are the principal feature around which the painting is composed.

pelling of the genre. Yet roses have not always been depicted evocatively, as if to capture their fragrance and ephemerality. The bed of a leaf, the vector of a stem, the inclination of a petal were rendered in antiquity, but only for purposes of decoration and botanical illustration. After the fourth century B.C., when Aristotle speculated about the soul of plants, herbal texts began to include colored illustrations of the physical and spiritual properties of flowers. The early Christians who escaped persecution by hiding in the catacombs of Rome adopted the rose as an emblem. Not daring to depict realistic images of their beliefs in their murals, they used the flower to signify charity, Christian love, and God's heavenly grace. By the first century A.D., artists were rendering roses, among other flowers, with closely observed depiction.

Since the rise of Christianity brought the demise of flower painting in the West, the art was practiced almost exclusively by non-Christian cultures, such as the Chinese, Persians, and Moslems, who were interested in the subject of flowers as other than religious or moral symbols. Flower painting was not revived in Europe until the twelfth century, when highly stylized images of roses and other blossoms reappeared as decorations and illustrations in herbals, Books of Hours, and the exquisitely calligraphed and illuminated texts created by monks for study and prayer. These volumes played so important a role in the daily life of the monasteries that a thirteeth-century monk lamented, "A monastery without books is like a state without resources, a table without food, a tree without leaves." Some manuscripts rendered in superb detail the daily tasks of the monk, others the rituals that physically enacted or represented the poetic, metaphoric text of the Scriptures. Still others were instructional, illustrating, for example, the construction of the letters of the alphabets in particular styles.

The rose, more than any other flower, developed a complex symbolic and emotional vocabulary. While the lily of the valley stood for humility, the violet for modesty, the daisy for mercy, and the white lily for purity, the rose embodied earthly love as well as the Virgin Mary's spiritual powers, and various kinds of roses were given even more specific connotations: *Rosa speciosa* was the valuable rose; *Rosa coeli,* the celestial rose; *Rosa spina carens,* the

OPPOSITE
The typically romantic rose is given uncommon intensity in Vincent van Gogh's
Vase of Pink Roses, *1890.*

thornless rose. By the fifteenth century, a worshiper gazing at the Mother of Christ might well have seen the roses that surrounded her either as an image of the thorny life of sorrow or as a visual incantation—a garland of rosaries.

By the Renaissance, the rose had come to represent female beauty, the brevity of love, and, to some extent, sexual passion. *Venus, Cupid, Folly and Time,* a strange, cautionary sixteenth-century painting by Bronzino, for example, shows Time holding a Blush China rose, which is thought to represent the threat of venereal diseases. By the end of that century, the rose also represented earth, the season spring, and, when depicted in a rose garden, the sense of smell. During the Elizabethan era, roses were known to have been used as an allegory for the swift passing of life. Though the rose was now acceptable as a symbolic image, the beauty of flowers was still considered "wholly inimitable and their sweetest service unrenderable by art." Even the great Western painters—Raphael, Leonardo, Michelangelo, Botticelli—employed the rose not as a subject in itself, but as a means of bringing greater beauty to their subjects.

Gradually, flower-filled landscapes and naturalistic floral sketches entered Western imagery. By the eighteenth century, riots of tempting innocence and charming naughtiness appeared in the work of artists such as Poussin, Boucher, and Fragonard. By the nineteenth century, any doubt about a flower's sensual and sexual implications had been dispelled. The rose, regularly used to epitomize the "lavishness of flowers," was equally associated with the physical beauty of the female body. In Renoir's famous theater painting, *La Loge,* the rose in the coquette's bosom, with its heavy flesh tones, represents what would be seen if the coquette were undressed. Other of Renoir's paintings in which "warm reds link the cheeks and lips to the roses" use the flower even more erotically.

≥∂

The tradition of still life painting evolved primarily during the sixteenth century in Italy and in the Netherlands, when, for the first time, what were called banquet paintings, breakfast paintings, or paintings with flower pots were considered appropriate artistic subjects. Until then, the still life had

OPPOSITE
Roses, Mexico *by Tina Modotti, 1925, brought $165,000 at Sotheby's, New York, in April 1991, making it the most expensive photograph ever sold at auction.*

been judged a lower exercise for a painter, and flowers meaningless as a principal subject. One critic claimed, "No mature artist should waste his brush on so lowly a model."

The "lesser" genres in the hierarchy of painting—landscape and still life—first expanded vigorously in the seventeenth century as a result of the influence of the formal art academies in the Netherlands. This "Golden Age" of still life was supported by the Calvinist church's ban on devotional imagery, which forced Dutch artists to emphasize secular subjects; and by a widespread interest in gardening, stimulated by the Dutch traders who returned from trips around the world with exotic flowers. The prosperous Dutch middle class, born of the free market conditions in a democratic culture, became a society of patrons who not only allowed, but encouraged artists to specialize in various genres.

Dutch flower paintings seduced the eye with their look of glossy wetness. Filled with bouquets of gloriously colored and unblemished blossoms, they represented an art of epicurean appetites. Not only did the aristocracy and the flourishing bourgeoisie find them

compelling, but for the first time in history, still life artists were kept on commission by the royal courts.

The term "still life," the portrayal of an ensemble of objects, derives from the Dutch term *stilleven*, which means life as well as model. The Dutch also

ABOVE
Roses in Glass *by Josef Sudek, c. 1950-54. (Houk Friedman Gallery, New York)*
OPPOSITE
On the Windowsill of My Studio *by Josef Sudek, c. 1951. (Laurence Miller Gallery, New York)*

used a specific word, *pronkstilleven*, to refer to a fancy still life, a sumptuous depiction of valuable objects, and rare fruit, foods, and flowers, whose purpose was to signify the riches and luxury available to the subjects' owner. Still lifes were also sought by those for whom fresh flowers were an unaffordable extravagance. Such a person might commission an "object portrait" of a rose as a means of keeping the flower in the house all year long.

Early floral portraits were approached much like a contemporary group portrait of people—each bloom was represented with equal emphasis and from the most advantageous angle. Absolute realism was not the intent, since, in what were known as botanical still lifes, flowers that bloomed in one season were juxtaposed with those that bloomed in another. Gradually, the natural realism of the ensemble replaced precise but imaginary compositions. In 1742, the flower painter Jan van Huysum complained that he could not finish a certain painting for he could no longer obtain a special kind of yellow rose during that year.

The concern for botanical accuracy eventually declined. Flowers began to be dramatized with an overt use of shadow. The poet Jacob Cats wrote, "Experience teaches us that many things appear to best advantage when not seen completely, but somehow veiled and in dark shadow."

Intentional obscurity also enabled the artist to describe the visual world while expressing hidden meanings. For, in still life, as in much of the history of Western art, the relationships between realism, symbolism, and moralizing content were manifold. Flowers, precious or rare objects, and other still life elements were called upon to represent biblical subjects: a table richly laden with fruits, vegetables, and full-blooming roses could appear in a Last Supper or in a picture of the Wedding at Cana as symbols of the riches of the life of the devout; a still life of antique rose-embossed objects might signify the treasures brought as gifts by the Magi.

As an emphasis on pure beauty grew, each new generation of still life artists confronted the genre's implicit representation of the fleeting moment. The poignancy of the ephemeral came to be the central subject of flower painting. Art historian Barbara Novak describes "the gentle urgency of the blossom and its imminent dissolution." The pre-Raphaelite

OPPOSITE
White Rosebud *by Josef Sudek, 1954. (Howard Greenberg Gallery, New York)*

painter Arthur Hughes lamented that painting roses was "a kind of match against time...they passing away so soon like all the lovely things under the sun...and as sensitive and beautiful."

The late-nineteenth-century French painter Edouard Manet, who, with his vivid sensual directness brought the art of still life into the modern era, produced a series of sixteen small flower paintings during the last months of his life. Marked by their frankness and painterly verve, they are the expressive opposite of the literal images produced two hundred years earlier by the first flower painters. They evoke the artist's own fragility as well as his fugitive excitement at the freshness of each bouquet. His *Roses in a Champagne Glass* luxuriates in the spontaneous impasto of petal against background. Painted quickly, in one or two sessions, it is alive with the pleasure Manet took both in the act of painting and in capturing the summer flower in winter—in defying time, in escaping the seasons.

While Manet was transmuting his physical suffering into paintings of roses, lilacs, and peonies, the practitioners of a new art form—photography—were just beginning to look at flowers. In the earliest nineteenth-century still life photographs, flowers are treated with a kind of specimen detachment. Later they were incorporated into the decorative profusions that served as backdrops to the subject of the photo. Even the Victorians, for whom the rose was a

Rose in Glass *by Josef Sudek, c. 1950-54. (Houk Friedman Gallery, New York)*

74

symbol of life incarnate and whose passion for growing them surpassed the French, photographed the flower without romance and drama.

Modern photographers have celebrated the rose as a life-cycle flower, as captivating in death as it is in life, as powerful in moments of commemoration as in moments of celebration. They have shown the rosebud to be as glamorous as a full blown rose; a rose about to open is seen as emotionally potent as a dying rose. They have photographed the stem, the thorn, the petal, and the flower's slightest changes from day to day. Unlike other flowers, no part of the rose is without visual interest. And unlike other flowers, the rose can be as compelling once it has died as it was in bloom, as Irving Penn's photographs demonstrate.

The photographer Peter C. Jones points out that still life photographs of roses take their meaning first from the light and then from the arrangement of other objects in the frame. "Even subtle changes in light have enormous impact on mood and meaning, and because the picture plane is so small, its content is all the more significant. A drop of dew or an insect on a petal will affect the mood of the subject, mak-ing the rose look either romantic or spooky. And if the surrounding objects look too perfect, the picture will quickly seem forced." Mr. Jones goes on to point out how, early on, the photographer must choose a direction—to shoot the rose in a composition that is either lush or sparse. "The photographer can either use a pure combination of flower and light to transcend the mundane or he or she can create a stage that suggests a story which takes its meaning from some attribute of the flower."

Josef Breitenbach, who associated with a number of photographers active in Germany and Paris during the 1920s and 30s—including Man Ray, André Kertész, Moholy-Nagy, and Lee Miller—developed a process for depicting aromas on film in much the way that Kerilian or infrared photography records heat on film. He began working with flowers and perfecting his technique after coming to the U.S. His series of photographs of the patterns of fragrance released by the rose are marked by a surreal beauty.

The Czechoslovakian photographer Josef Sudek expanded the parameters of the photographic still life by shooting roses on his windowsill. The simultaneous indoor/outdoor dimension of the pictures is

rare for the art form, which one traditionally associates with a wholly interior setting.

The crush of fragile beauty in *Roses, Mexico* by the Mexican photographer Tina Modotti works as an almost abstract portrait of the flower, a picture of vulnerability, of disturbing delicacy. The image represents a greater concern for power and emotion than the photograph of roses, to which this alludes, taken by Edward Steichen forty years earlier.

Sun-splashed and romantic, the still lifes of roses by Alex Gotfryd combine an exquisite selection of soft and beautiful objects with flowers in near and full bloom. His use of a high grain texturally unifies his images and further softens their lushness. Gotfryd's photographs, like Manet's flower paintings, were the last works of the artist's career and serve as a testament to his exceptional graciousness and bonhomie.

PHOTOGRAPHS ON PAGES 76–81
Renowned book designer Alex Gotfryd was asked to make a series of rose still lifes especially for this book. He completed the series in January 1991 shortly before his death.
(Lieberman & Saul Gallery, New York)

Garden Roses

❧

As he sketched in the garden of the Persian palace Negauristan, the nineteenth-century English artist Ker Porter found his hand moving with extraordinary fluidity. Everywhere his eye moved, he glimpsed a flowering vista, an allée, a pool, or walkway more beautiful than any he'd seen in all his years of travels. At last, drunk with the splendor of the scene and the heady sweetness of roses in the air, he was about to retire when he was struck by the sight of two twenty-foot rose trees, their thick trunks completely concealed by thousands of flowers in every stage of blooming. Quickly but meticulously, Ker Porter rendered the remarkable sight and then reached for his writing tablet. "A most delicious spot, this fairyland. Indeed I may call it the very garden of Beauty and the Beast, for the eye and the smell are not the only senses regaled by the presence of roses. The ear is enchanted by the wild and beautiful notes of multitudes of nightingales whose warblings seem to increase in melody and softness, with the unfolding of their favourite flowers verifying the lyric: 'When the roses fade, when the charms of the bower are passed away, the fond tale of the nightingale no longer animates the scene.'"

Like garden roses grown throughout the world, those captured by Ker Porter's pen were the product of a uniquely intertwined social history and horticultural evolution. An account of the rose's cultivation reveals a peculiar mixture of patronage and banishment, of ravishing beauty and bitter politics, of poetic exaltation and chronic dispute.

OPPOSITE
Photograph by Peter C. Jones of a bouquet of 'New Dawn' roses crowning heart-shaped stems on a wall in coastal Rhode Island, 1987.
OVERLEAF
Roses in the Mist *by Lizzie Himmel, 1989, East Hampton, Long Island.*

Ker Porter wrote that "in no country of the world {did} the rose grow in such perfection as in Persia: in no country {was} it so cultivated, and prized by the natives. Their gardens and courts {were} crowded with its plants, their rooms ornamented with vases, filled with its gathered bunches, and every bath strewn with the full-blown flowers, plucked from the ever-replenished stems. Even the humblest individual, who paid a piece of copper money for a few whiffs of a rose, felt a double enjoyment when he found it stuck with a bud from his dear native tree!"

The Persians considered the rose the most beautiful of flowers and called it *gul*, which also became the general term for "flower." A rose garden is called *gulistan*, a flower garden *gulzar*, a bouquet *guldasta*, and the song of the nightingale is the *gulbang*, the flower cry. Rose water, traditionally kept in beautiful glass containers to be sprinkled upon guests on their arrival, is *gulab*. In Lord Byron's poem "The Bride of Abydos"

> She snatched the urn wherein was mix'd
> The Persian Atar-gul's perfume
> And Sprinkled all its odours o'er
> The pictur'd roof and marble floor.

Roses of many colors were reported by travelers in Persia as early as the eleventh century. Among them was the "hundred-petaled rose," which was also recorded at Isfahan in the seventeenth century. It was likely grown on plantations where thousands of pounds of the flower were gathered each day for the preparation of rose attar. Even today, great rose fields can be found in Kashan.

ABOVE AND OPPOSITE
Because of the Islamic prohibition on human depiction, flowers, especially the rose, found frequent representation in religious and sacred art, as in these illuminations.

In the sixteenth century Sulyeman the Magnificent, ruler of the Ottomans, employed thousands of gardeners to tend his forty flower gardens in which tulips, carnations, flowering trees, and roses were grown. The frequent depictions of the sultan smelling a rose symbolize his union with Mohammed, who is believed to have said, "When I was taken up to heaven, some of my sweat fell on the earth and from it sprang the rose, and whoever would smell my scent, let him smell the rose." Roses were planted beneath the windows of Ottoman palaces so that their fragrance could fill the harem rooms, and rows of potted roses were kept in mosques to enhance the worshipers' sense of the Prophet's presence.

In India, during the Mughal rule, whole gardens were devoted to the worship of individual flowers, principally the lilac, the tulip, and the rose. The Gulabi Bagh at Lahore, for example, was a walled rose garden whose flowering beds were said to "cause the Tulip Garden's jealousy." As with the Ottomans and other Moslems, the idea of Paradise for the Mughals was a place where angels, gentle beasts, bright birds, and glittering fish lived in perfect harmony among the sweetest of blooms, an

OPPOSITE AND ABOVE
Eighteenth-century Indian miniatures illustrate the rose as a symbol of love and allude to its place in Indian gardens. According to legend, roses were floated each night in the reflecting pool of the Taj Mahal and skimmed away each morning, leaving behind waters perfumed for the bath of the Shah Jehan's beloved.

image which underlaid their artistic world. Miniature portraits of Mughal emperors and their nobles often show a figure standing in a rose garden with a perfect stem in hand, the flower—and the figure—painted with precise, delicious skill. Carpets, tiles, fruit plates, rose water vessels, and wine cups also bore paradisiacal motifs. Borders of embroidered roses edged soft Kashmir shawls; bouquets of roses were stitched in gold on muslins; and rugs and hangings were woven with depictions of garden avenues planted with cypresses, fruit trees, and rose bushes.

Most Mughal gardens were enormous in scale, with water running through narrow channels to give life and character to the broad stone walkways, and with cooling rows of cypresses to soften the glare of sunshine on white marble. Rose bushes bordered raised walkways, the fallen petals cushioning the paths of the visitor or worshiper. The gardens of the shahs included bathing courts with marble basins as wide as sixty or seventy feet, filled, as one palace scribe recounted, "with the clearest water, sparkling in the sun, for its only canopy was the vault of heaven. Rose trees were clustered near them and, at times, their waving branches threw beautifully quivering shade over the brilliant pools." The water that flowed through the spring-fed basins remained cool, always at a temperature that renewed the body's vigor and refreshed the air, "which the sun's influence and the thousand roses breathing around might otherwise have rendered oppressive with their incense."

In Kashmir the festival of the rose is still celebrated at the Shalimar Bagh, where pink roses grow beside the pools, red roses fill the parterres, and yellow roses climb the gray-green walls of the Hall of Public Audience and "hang their soft heads down-

ABOVE LEFT
A hybrid tea bud, 'Grand Siècle,' beginning to unfold.
ABOVE RIGHT
A hybrid tea bloom, 'Die Welt,' characterized by luminescent petals darker at the edges.
OPPOSITE
Hybrid tea roses, including Pascali, Lancôme, and 'Charles de Gaulle.' (All Lanny Provo)

ward in clusters from the carved cedar cornice. Climbing roses twine about the painted wooden pillars, and nod their creamy flowers through the opening of the lattice," while rose-scented breezes mingle with the drifting fountain spray.

❧

In the West, the Gallica, or French rose, was preeminent during the Roman Empire. The oldest identified rose, it has red, pink, or purple flowers and dark green, rough-textured foliage. Sometime during the Middle Ages, it was crossed with a wild rose to produce the damasks, which are best known for their fragrance. Medium to large in size, they have drooping or arching branches and are still grown commercially in the Near East for the production of attar, a fragrant oil. The flowers are medium-sized, semi-double or double, and appear in large clusters in shades of white and pink.

Damasks eventually were crossed with the species Rosa canina to produce the albas—tall, dense, hardy, and pest- and disease-resistant roses that bloom only once a year. Their leaves are blue-green, and their medium-sized petals are pink or white, clustered and

OPPOSITE
A double pale pink shrub rose trails along a stone wall. (Lizzie Himmel)
ABOVE
A Lady Picking Roses, *by Wynn Richards, c. 1925. (Howard Greenberg Gallery)*
OVERLEAF
A sparse climbing pink polyantha rose just beginning to unfold. (Lizzie Himmel)

deliciously fragrant. In seventeenth-century Holland, the alba produced the favored centifolia, or cabbage rose, so named because its hundred or more petals overlap like cabbage leaves. It is also called the Provence rose because it was once grown in that region of France. A sweetly fragrant flower that clusters once a year on slender, arching branches with crinkled leaves, the centifolia ranges in color from white to deep red. Its progeny is the moss rose, a highly fragrant flower whose perfume is emitted from the small, mossy, sticky red or green glands that appear on the stem and leaves. Its petals are white, pink, red, or purple, and it blooms only once a season, usually later than other roses.

These five families dominated Western rose gardening from the time of the Roman Empire through the Enlightenment. This *ancien régime* of the rose ended in 1789 when the China rose, *R. chinensis,* which had the ability to flower more than once a season, was introduced in Europe. The first of these recurring, or remontant, roses was the Portland, a cross between a China rose, the "Autumn Damask," and *Rosa gallica.* Sturdy, upright plants, their double flowers are extremely fragrant and bloom all summer.

But the most popular of this type was the Bourbon, a naturally occurring hybrid found on the Île de Bourbon, a small island near Mauritius in the Indian Ocean, in 1823 and sent back to Paris. This rose, Napoleonic in bearing, combined the remontant trait with the beauty of Old World blooms. It was the favorite of the Empress Josephine, and through her passionate cultivation became the preeminent ornamental flower of the nineteenth century.

Although roses were grown even before biblical times in the Holy Land—for the purpose of making rose water—the first serious cultivation of the flower there was not begun for thousands of years, when, during the 1850s, a settlement near the southern end of the Sea of Galilee devoted itself to growing the *shoshana* (the Hebrew word for rose).

In 1867, a French breeder produced what is considered by many to be the first hybrid tea—a continually blooming rose called "La France." It grew on a petite bush, had a long, shapely bud, and was similar to the China roses but with larger, fuller flowers. The double flowers are pastel with almost translucent petals and a fresh, tea-like fragrance. Growing on graceful plants with long, pointed buds, their

PRECEDING PAGES
An island planting of pink and white floribunda roses surrounded by ball-shaped boxwood. (Lizzie Himmel)

classic, high-centered form is regarded today as the quintessence of the rose.

The development of the tea rose initiated the division of the rose into two categories: old garden roses, those that were in existence before 1867; and modern roses, those that came into existence after that date, in which varieties of every color except true blue can be found. These two categories are further broken down into types designated by species background or blooming characteristics. Climber, floribunda, grandiflora, hybrid tea, miniature, polyantha, rambler, and shrub make up the the modern rose's primary classifications.

Like many other events in the rose's history, the categorizing of the flower became a source of enduring controversy. Graham Stuart Thomas, the English rose grower and author of *Old Shrub Roses* extolled the "lasciviousness, luxuriousness, pedigree, and sexuality" of old garden roses. He lauded them for being hardier and less susceptible to plagues, and for possessing stronger, richer, more varied perfumes— spice, myrrh, cinnamon, clove, apples, orange, and banana-like scents—than modern roses. "Sumptuous and ravishing," he wrote, "there is just a suspicion of

flesh pink in {the} half-open buds." Fanciers of modern roses take issue with claims of superiority such as Thomas's, pointing out that their roses have different but equal virtues: they bloom all season long, rather than just heavily once a summer (with an occasional encore), and their spectrum is wider than that of the Old Rose, which is limited to a softer, subtler palette, ranging from white to pink and red.

By the end of the nineteenth century, the Victorian spirit of invention and competitive energy spurred rose breeders to develop hybrids that would appeal to the growing middle class. The ensuing changes were revolutionary: the flower diminished from a sprawling shrub to a bush in order to accommodate the constraints of smaller gardens; and the shape was modified to satisfy the contemporary obsession with the prim, just-barely-opened bloom, a response, in part, to Victorian flower-show criteria. Rose growers sought tight, high-centered blooms and officially turned their backs on the old garden varieties, whose blossoms were flattened like architectural rosettes or overblown like petticoats.

Soon, traditionalists were expressing their disdain for hybrid teas as a mark of both common sense and refined taste. Vita Sackville-West, for example, found them insufficiently subtle, too highly colored, and altogether bourgeois. Another rose authority described the modern rose's flower as "a jumble of petals of no particular form." In the words of the writer Michael Pollan, the rose had become "dwarfed, dubbed with a series of undignified names, dressed up in ridiculous hues, and often made to stand shoulder to shoulder in a crowd, the glory of its individual blooms subordinated to a mass effect, to a crude 'blaze of color.'" While hybrid breeders gloried in the cultivation of ever more colorful, perpetually blooming variations, fanciers of the old rose took refuge in restrained good taste. "It should be remembered that a rose garden can never be called gorgeous," advised the English landscape designer Gertrude Jekyll. "The term is quite unfitting." Several decades later, the American writer Gertrude Stein had the last word: "A rose is a rose is a rose."

ૐ

Magnificent public rose gardens of great diversity can be found in every part of the world. Some are devoted to particular varieties, others to specific forms of landscape design, while still others recapitulate the history of the flower. Unfortunately, few historical illustrations of the original early gardens exist, and we must rely on verbal descriptions and aerial schemes to imagine what they looked like.

Among the most extraordinary of the world's rose gardens is the Bagatelle in Paris, with more than 10,000 rose bushes of over 1,500 varieties. Originally part of an estate owned by Marie Antoinette and later by Napoleon, this two-and-one-half acre garden was acquired in 1905 by the City of Paris at the instigation of the Conservator of Parks, who happened to be a friend of Claude Monet. The Impressionst painter's influence can be seen in daring juxtapositions of color. A dramatic range of garden devices emphasizes this vivid profusion: roses are planted as ground cover, in bushes, and as ramblers on swags; pillar roses are grown on conifers, and standard roses with smaller roses planted beneath; there are weeping roses, shrub roses, pergola roses, roses planted individually in lawns bordered with miniature box hedges, roses

OPPOSITE
A silk rose on a sunbonnet creates a floral tableau in a southern garden of full-blown roses. (Carlos Domenech)

View of the Cranford Rose Garden at the Brooklyn Botanic Garden. Front roses are modern pink shrub 'Bonica,' peach-colored shrub 'Fred Loads,' and white hybrid perpetual 'Frau Karl Druschki.' Wild and old roses grow in the outer borders. (Christine Douglas)

Center beds in the Cranford Rose Garden planted with fragrant white low growing polyantha shrub 'Clotilde Soupert.' On the pavilion are climbing roses: red 'Grand Hotel,' white 'Dr. Van Fleet,' and pink 'Aloha.' (Christine Douglas)

arranged formally in circular beds, and roses grown in bands to frame parts of the garden.

Many of the roses planted in the garden of the Château de Bagatelle were provided by Jules Gravereaux, the owner of the Roseraie de l'Hay-les-Roses, another of France's splendid rose gardens. In 1892, when Gravereaux first purchased his estate south of Paris, one hundred different roses grew there. By 1900 there were three thousand varieties. Today, the five-acre garden overlooking the River Bievre includes a section for cut rose varieties; beds illustrating the history of the garden rose; collections of notable hybrids, of roses of the Middle and Far East, and of Gallica roses, the roses of the Empress

ABOVE LEFT
Rosa spinosissima altaica, *a lightly fragrant species introduced in 1820 from western Asia.*
ABOVE RIGHT
Rosa chinensis minima 'Rosie,' *which grows on one-foot miniature bushes.*
OPPOSITE
Blush Damask, a highly fragrant soft pink rose used in potpourri. (All Christine Douglas)

Josephine's Malmaison (a garden Gravereaux helped reestablish with 197 varieties known during the lifetime of the Empress); a decorative rose garden surrounding a reflecting pool; new hybrids from French breeders and similar collections from foreign hybridizers; collections of wild roses and tea roses; and a "theater of the rose"—a setting for concerts, recitals, ballets, and fetes staged in honor of the flower.

Not surprisingly, outstanding rose gardens can be found throughout England. For serious rose breeders, the Royal National Rose Society lists gardens whose flowers have passed their scrutiny, including their test garden at St. Albans. The National Trust publishes lists of its properties that include rose gardens, such as Mottisfont Abbey in Hampshire, a twelfth-century Augustinian priory that has a walled garden stocked with old fashioned roses. The Royal Horticultural Society's garden is located at Wisley, and Sissinghurst Castle in Kent, whose gardens were planned by Vita Sackville-West, is the stage for a variety of old and new roses. In London, the rose enthusiast can stroll at leisure through Queen Mary's Garden in Regent's Park, the Royal Botanic Garden, and the garden at Kew.

One of the most unusually designed rose gardens in the world is found in Westbroekpark in The Hague, Netherlands. Paths wind through lawns in which three sections of roses are planted in beds of three different configurations—oblong, square, and triangular. This arrangement of twenty thousand plants, representing 350 varieties, makes it possible to compare the effects of massing different varieties.

The three-tiered octagonal rose garden known as the Parc de la Grange in Geneva lies on the south side of Lake Leman, not far from a floral clock and a magnificent plume of water that jets so high into the air it can be seen from passing planes. Created immediately after World War II to give work to jobless citizens, it is decorated with pergolas, fountains, and pools, and planted with 12,000 roses of 200 varieties. Rose trees are grown at the corners of some of the beds, some bearing flowers that hang like parasols and others with upright stems that reach for the sky. Clipped conical evergreens give contrast of color, texture, and form. The garden is illuminated at night, and it is used as a stage for plays based on rose themes.

Five thousand roses of one thousand varieties are

cultivated at the Rosarium at the Villa Reale at Monza, the headquarters of the Italian Rose Society, just north of Milan. In Rome, four thousand bushes in groups of five are crowned with a magnificent backdrop of climbing roses in the Roseto de Roma, sited in a natural amphitheater.

In Spain, a country known for its love of the rose, exceptional rose gardens can be found in Cordoba, Granada, Valencia, Seville, and Madrid. North of the former royal palace, near the road from Madrid to La Coruña, is the Rosaleda del Parque del Oeste which contains what is probably the country's most impressive rose display.

Chandigarh, the capital of the Punjab in India, is known as the "City of Roses" and has an ideal climate and soil for growing the flower. Its thirty-acre Zakir Rose Garden contains sixty thousand plants in a uniquely informal design that includes four sections: a Museum of the Rose, a collection of the best known rose varieties arranged in beds and with an open space for celebrating rose festivals; a display area with three hundred large beds, each planted with more than one hundred plants of a single exhibition variety, as well as a rosewood garden for the ramblers of various colors and a moonlight garden with only pure white roses; a scent garden for roses with a high oil content whose flowers are used for the extraction of oil and rose water; and a "laboratory" garden for hybridizing, grafting, and other experimentation.

The largest garden in the world devoted primarily to roses is the American Rose Center in Shreveport, Louisiana, comprised of more than forty individual rose gardens set along woodland paths. The Boerner Botanical Garden outside Milwaukee has one of this nation's finest rose gardens. Unusual settings characterize the Buchardt Gardens in Victoria, Canada, where the garden was dug on the site of a former mine, and the Chicago Botanic Garden in Glencoe, a series of islands built on a former marsh. More majestic is the International Rose Test Garden in Washington Park in Portland, Oregon. Like Chandigarh, warm days, cool nights, and deep fertile soil make Portland an ideal location for growing roses and account for its title, "The City of Roses." The garden's ten thousand rose bushes are terraced into five acres of hillside beneath the towering Mt. Hood.

The Brooklyn Botanic Garden, an urban oasis by contrast, has five thousand plants of over fifteen hundred varieties in its one-acre Cranford Rose Garden. Equally dramatic in context are New York's Queens Botanical Garden and the New York Botanical Gardens' Peggy Rockefeller Rose Garden. Originally designed in 1915, the plans for the landscape lay dormant for more than seventy years. Following the English fashion, climbing roses on the central arbor as well as on the perimeter trellises are intertwined with clematis. There are also shaped beds of miniature roses, beds of hybrid teas and grandifloras planted along paths, and separate beds of floribundas. Old fashioned shrub roses and newer rose varieties are also displayed.

The concept of a municipal garden, developed and maintained by public funds, was born in the late nineteenth century. Not far from New York's rose gardens is the Hartford Rose Garden in Hartford, Connecticut, the first municipal rose garden created in the U.S. and the centerpiece of Elizabeth Park. Begun in 1896, it predates even the Rosarie in the Bagatelle. The central garden is a perfect square with an entrance in the middle of each side leading into four fourteen-foot-wide turf walkways. Narrower diagonal paths lead to corner entrances. Seventy-eight wood and iron arches, covered with ramblers and climbers, decorate the walks, which intersect at a rustic summer house surrounded by rugosa roses. The rest of the garden includes 132 rectangular beds, each containing a single variety. Suffused with the romance of its long vistas and arched pathways, the Hartford Rose Garden is a favorite spot for bridal portraits. It was also a daily inspiration for the poet Wallace Stevens, who walked through the park every workday.

OPPOSITE
Rosa gallica officinalis, *the oldest cultivated gallica, is called the 'Apothecary' rose because for centuries it was believed to cure many ailments and was made into syrups and powders. Some consider it the most famous rose. It is highly fragrant and grows on bushes to three and a half feet. (Christine Douglas)*

Rooms with Roses

As they strolled down the *promenade des jardins* of Versailles, King Louis XV and his mistress, Madame du Barry, marveled at the palace's extravagant landscape of trees, flowers, and plants collected from throughout the French empire. The setting, used frequently as a site for theatricals, concerts, and al fresco supper parties, was also ideal for private rendezvous. After lingering in the fragrance garden, so intensely scented that even a blindfolded person could find his way along the avenues of orange and lemon trees and the rows of Judean jasmines and lilacs, the couple arrived at the rose garden. There they found roses spilling from urns, climbing trellises, and showering petals upon their path. Enchanted, Madame du Barry confided to the King her desire to have her private chambers made as beautiful as this bower. Soon a lavish canopy of rose-patterned silk covered her bed, carved rose garlands climbed the bed posts, and curtains embroidered with patterns of cascading roses billowed from her windows.

At the beginning of each season, the matching sets of window dressings, bed covers, and slipcovers in all the private quarters throughout the palace were replaced. Though Madame du Barry's fabrics changed from silk to linen to brocade to tapestry, their decorative motifs varied only between the simple wild rose and the many-petaled bloom of the cultivated rose. The rose decor so pleased her that, upon the completion of her new pavilions, she commissioned Jean-Honoré Fragonard to paint a series of decorative panels featuring roses.

OPPOSITE
"Fleurs en 18 Couleurs," 1855 block print by Jules Desfosse. (Leslie Jean-Bart)
OVERLEAF
Rose-patterned wallpaper provides a sweet background to an ornate frame. (David Phelps)
PAGES 114–115
"Rose and Floral Wreath," an English glazed cotton, c. 1880. (Leslie Jean-Bart)

torical and exotic scenes or still lifes, were manufactured in long, continuous lengths. In almost all of these early wallpapers, roses were among the most frequently depicted flower.

By the nineteenth century, even the British Houses of Parliament were being decorated with rose-patterned wallpapers, such as the rose-and-coronet wallpaper designed by Augustus Pugin. During the Victorian era, rose-patterned fabrics and wallpapers relieved the dark look of English parlors crowded with overstuffed upholstery, shrouded tables, and fringed runners. Later, the influential English furniture and textile designer William Morris, whose ideas on design and manufacture animated the Arts and Crafts Movement, further liberated these rooms with the naturalism of his rose and other floral patterned wallpapers, textiles, carpets, and tapestries, incorporating the natural coloring and growth patterns of plants in his work. He chose a rose-on-trellis pattern for his first block-printed wallpaper.

The rose was a favorite decorative motif of Morris's Scottish contemporary, Charles Rennie Mackintosh, whose fluid, attenuated version of the flower appears in his furniture, window glass, wall

ABOVE
Detail of an early-20th-century American wallcovering.
OPPOSITE
Detail of a mid-19th-century French wallcovering.
OVERLEAF
Detail of a 19th-century wallcovering.

panels, and artifacts. His sketchbooks show linear studies of "A Moss Rose," "Faded Roses," a "Yellow Rose," and "White Roses."

⁊⥁

Chintz enjoyed a return to popularity during the early part of this century. Revived for its look of casual elegance, the fabric received its blessing first from America's most fashionable decorators. Elsie de Wolfe used it lavishly in New York's Colony Club. Rose Cumming, who started her company in 1917, shocked the decorating establishment by mixing chintz with silks and satins, thereby elevating it into the world of formality. And Dorothy Draper made overscaled cabbage rose chintz her trademark. Forty years ago, the English decorator John Fowler, of Colefax and Fowler, reinstated chintz in England along with Geoffrey Bennison, who printed faded-looking rose and other flower patterns on expensive linens. The contemporary heirs to these arbiters of high fashion—Nancy Lancaster, Sister Parish, Mark Hampton, Mario Buatta, Keith Irvine, and Georgina Fairholme—employ great fecund chintzes filled with roses and other flowers as an essential element in their English country house style interiors.

Unpretentiously impressive, the English country house look derives its tranquil grandeur from a sense of well-worn pedigree, as if Victorian splendor had

ABOVE
Fragment of a 19th-century wallcovering.
OPPOSITE
Detail of Scalamandre's "Philippe de la Salle Rose," reproduction of a Louis XVI lampas.

relaxed into a mood of slightly tattered elegance. Comfort and the cool coordination of color and design intimate the presence of an English garden just beyond the doors. Fine furniture in casual but sensible arrangements and a seemingly unstudied assemblage of paints, papers, and natural fabrics, especially rose chintzes, impart an aura of civility and warmth.

Mario Buatta learned directly from John Fowler how to combine English design with American know-how. He turns to roses, both fresh and patterned, as a means of personalizing a room. Esteemed as a colorist and renowned as "the prince of chintz," Mr. Buatta melds the preferences he gleans from a client with his own well honed sensibilities. "I like flowers and my clients like flowers, especially roses. Whether massed in vases or on fabric, they enhance a room's beauty. It's that simple."

The interior designer Ron Grimaldi, of Rose Cumming, admires the rose's great flexibility. "It knows no limits: all sorts of looks are complemented by rose fabrics—French, Italian, English. And they work comfortably in every kind of room. You can use a rose chintz anywhere—as a table skirt, a pillow—it goes with everything." Although he considers the flower "luscious and delicate, the full blown expression of romance," Mr. Grimaldi does not find it limited to the feminine. He applied a wallpaper of overblown cabbage roses on a dark brown background in a man's bedroom and used other rose patterns in a formal library. Like the founder of his firm, he does not hesitate to use a curtain of rose chintz in a room filled with contrasting fabrics. "Rose Cumming was a woman of great flair and innovation. She worked purely by instinct and did what no one had ever thought to do before: she combined blues and greens in the same room, she mixed different weights of fabrics together, but, most of all, she broke from the idea that you could only use chintz informally. She mixed satins, silks, and lots of rose chintz together to give rooms a look of opulence."

Gary Hager, an interior designer at Parish-Hadley, finds it effective to fill a room with rose patterns because "everyone responds to the flower. They know it from their own imaginations, they know it from their own experiences of love. And when people are familiar with something, they're not afraid of it. Familiarity breeds comfort." When selecting a rose wallpaper, fabric, and/or carpet for a

PRECEDING PAGES AND OPPOSITE
David Kleinberg of Parish-Hadley Associates chose a rose-patterned antique Bessarabian carpet and obsessively applied rose-patterned cotton chintzes to give a bedroom a mood of elegant vivacity. (John Hall)
OVERLEAF
Rose-patterned carpet from Stark Carpet lightens the formality of a library. (Peter Vitale)

As an indulgence of sheer luxury, the architect Whitney Warren was commissioned to transform a hotel ballroom into a replica of the Hall of Mirrors at Versailles for a party given in New York early in the 1900s. After covering the ballroom ceiling with a sky blue canopy, he banked its walls with thousands of rose bushes and scattered throughout the room more live bushes in full bloom, their branches twined with small glowing lights. On the floor below, where the guests descended for supper after the entertainment, he decorated rooms to resemble tents on the grounds of the French palace, and covered the parquet floors with a green lawn and trellised rose bushes wound with rainbow-colored lights. Elsie de Wolfe, who attended the *fête,* costumed herself in a copy of an eighteenth-century gown with enormous sleeves gathered at the elbow with circles of satin roses. Although she ranked the rose-strewn ball as one of the most grandly decorated affairs in her experience of New York society, it had unfortunate consequences for the host. The focus on his extravagance led to investigations of his financial "mismanagements," bringing about his resignation from his businesses and, ultimately, he fled the country.

room, Mr. Hager regulates the concentration of roses in a room according to the density of the rose images in the fabrics, floor and wallcoverings. Generally, however, he likes to apply representations of the flower lightly, "to insure they don't get lost in the decoration, to be sure you can 'see' them."

Other designers indulge a passion for the actual flower. The couturier Valentino insists that a bower of roses fill his home every day of the year, even when he is away. "It's an obvious extravagance," he admits, "but I like the thought that my house is alive with roses even when I'm absent."

ABOVE
Chair covered in "Sackville-West," a fabric by Rose Cumming.
OPPOSITE
"Tudor Rose," pattern made in both fabric and wallpaper by Rose Cumming.

OPPOSITE
Roses in bloom and in potpourri animate an Oriental tableau by Leon Amar.
ABOVE LEFT
"Haddon Hall," a Bruschwig & Fils chintz, appears in a highly feminine boudoir.
ABOVE RIGHT
Roses add romance to Leon Amar's exotic salon. (All Peter Vitale).

137

PRECEDING PAGES
Roses in an Aubusson rug and needlepoint settee in a Maureen Sullivan Stemberg interior.
ABOVE
A settee is covered in a rose-patterned Victorian cotton.
OPPOSITE
A bedroom reminiscent of Madame du Barry's boudoir. (All Peter Vitale)

140

ABOVE
*A classical bust is counterpoised against a fauteuil covered in an equally elegant
rose-patterned fabric. (George Ross)*
OPPOSITE
*A rose obsession is expressed in the choice of a porcelain pitcher and wallcovering deco-
rated with the flower. (David Phelps)*

ABOVE
*A single rose lends a touch of beauty to a reading niche in the bedroom of a
New York City apartment.*
OPPOSITE
*Bountiful arrangements of roses are the centerpieces of a setting whose grandeur is
established by the John Singer Sargent portrait at rear.
(Both Lizzie Himmel)*

torical and exotic scenes or still lifes, were manufactured in long, continuous lengths. In almost all of these early wallpapers, roses were among the most frequently depicted flower.

By the nineteenth century, even the British Houses of Parliament were being decorated with rose-patterned wallpapers, such as the rose-and-coronet wallpaper designed by Augustus Pugin. During the Victorian era, rose-patterned fabrics and wallpapers relieved the dark look of English parlors crowded with overstuffed upholstery, shrouded tables, and fringed runners. Later, the influential English furniture and textile designer William Morris, whose ideas on design and manufacture animated the Arts and Crafts Movement, further liberated these rooms with the naturalism of his rose and other floral patterned wallpapers, textiles, carpets, and tapestries, incorporating the natural coloring and growth patterns of plants in his work. He chose a rose-on-trellis pattern for his first block-printed wallpaper.

The rose was a favorite decorative motif of Morris's Scottish contemporary, Charles Rennie Mackintosh, whose fluid, attenuated version of the flower appears in his furniture, window glass, wall

ABOVE
Detail of an early-20th-century American wallcovering.
OPPOSITE
Detail of a mid-19th-century French wallcovering.
OVERLEAF
Detail of a 19th-century wallcovering.

The first panel, called *Storming the Citadel*, portrays a lover leaping over a wall of roses. The second, *The Pursuit*, shows him offering his mistress a rose, which she rejects in mock horror. In the third, *The Declaration of Love*, he has won her affections and holds her in his rosy arms. The fourth panel shows *The Lover Crowned* by his mistress with a garland of roses.

Madame du Barry was one of a number of persons of great style and imagination with a taste for decorating rooms with roses. From the eighteenth century to the present day, the flower has been a prolific motif in wall coverings, upholstery, pillows, and carpets.

Madame de Pompadour, Madame du Barry's predecessor and also a lover of roses, was one of the Western world's great patrons of beauty. She exercised her intelligence and taste not only to amuse, entertain, and assist the King, but also to achieve her highest desire: "Every day I wish to make the world a more beautiful place than I found it." And with this aim, she raised the decorative arts—furniture, porcelain, bronze, and wall paneling—to a high art form.

Together with Louis XV, Madame de Pompadour bought or built fourteen major residences, all of which required complete decoration. Her taste for intimacy

was elegant yet revolutionary. Equally radical was her insistence that everything in her rooms fit together harmoniously. She commissioned seating that was not only sensuous, but was also the first furniture in modern Europe intended to be comfortable. The brilliance and extravagance of the rococo, her favored style, with its curvilinear floral motifs and its arabesques of roses, quickly swept the courts of Europe.

Even before the rococo, during the second half of the seventeenth century, a bright cotton fabric printed with lively roses and other highly patterned floral designs became the fashion in France and England. Manufactured in India, where it was called "chittes,"

PAGES 116–117
An 18th-century French silk brocaded chasuble, c. 1770–80. (Scalamandre)

OPPOSITE AND ABOVE
Designs of a rose on a thorny stem, colorful flocked roses, and roses growing in the wild were included in a sample book of hand-blocked wallcoverings by Jules Desfosse for the Exposition Universale of 1855. (Leslie Jean-Bart)

chintz was fast-printed in not fewer than five colors and usually glazed. As Indo-European trade expanded, the demand for the flowered fabric grew so passionate that the leaders of France and England's textile industries were moved to protest its import: The English passed an act of Parliament banning the importation of all decorative materials from the Orient, and the French textile industry pressured the government to pass a law forbidding the importation, wearing, and use of chintz. The bans, naturally, had an opposite effect, creating an obsession with chintz, which was called "indiennes" by the French. For the next hundred years, contraband chintzes were smuggled into Europe, and chintz spies lurked everywhere. The English actor David Garrick publicly bemoaned the seizure by customs officials of his wife's rose chintz bed hangings. Along with many English gentlemen, he himself used chintz in the long robes known as "banyans" that he wore when entertaining at home. Finally, around 1850, only after it could be mass-produced in Europe, chintz fell from its position as an exotic luxury.

Ever since it appeared in Europe in the fifteenth century, wallpaper has been used by those who could not afford the tapestries, painted cloths, murals, stucco work, leather and paneling that were applied to the walls of the nobility and wealthy merchants. The rose was one of the first floral motifs regularly reproduced on wallpaper. In a typical sixteenth-century English wallpaper, a Tudor rose surrounds the heraldic arms of Queen Elizabeth I. The crest appears in the center of the sheet, with a section positioned in each corner, the complete flower being formed by the junction of adjacent sheets. The French artist Jean Papillon Père was among the first to make patterns on paper printed from carved wood blocks that matched in repeating units when the sheets of paper were joined. Tiny Tudor roses also appear on seventeenth-century wallpapers, called "Spanish stitch" papers, whose designs imitate stitchery.

Nearly a century later, just prior to the French Revolution, Jean-Baptiste Revéillon printed sheets of wallpaper in one continuous length. Garlands of roses now stretched in unbroken swags from one end of a room to the other. However, it was not until the nineteenth century that "papier peints," hand-blocked wallpapers that looked like paintings of his-

OPPOSITE

"Rococo Rose print," 19th-century English plain-weave glazed cotton. (Leslie Jean-Bart)

PAGES 146–147
A bouquet of roses tossed casually (or perhaps hastily by a lover) into a chair casts an aura of mystery upon a room.

PAGE 148
Roses form part of the lavish decoration of a dessert corner at a holiday entertainment.

PAGE 149
In a room whose somewhat casual tone is established by the exposed brick wall, a bouquet of roses ties together the eclectic mix of fine accessories.

OPPOSITE
A crystal vial hung by a chain next to a fireplace serves as a clever and unusual bud vase for two stems of roses.

PAGES 152-153
A bouquet of carnations, iris, bourbons, teas, and Portland roses is centered between candlesticks and green-glazed ceramic roses.

PAGE 154
A bunch of cosmos and snapdragons is counterpoised against a jumble of rose-patterned pillows in a Long Island weekend house.

PAGE 155
A bunch of fully opened, highly fragrant hybrid tea 'Mojave' roses, named for their coloration which resembles the desert at sunset.

(All Lizzie Himmel)

ABOVE
A single rose punctuates a still life of dollhouse-sized miniatures set in and on an antique pie safe.

OPPOSITE
Roses from among the 1,100 species and varieties of the flower complete the composition of an elegant tableau. (Both Lizzie Himmel)

Illustration Credits

❧

PAGE 2: Water color on paper, courtesy the Metropolitan Museum of Art, New York, Rogers Fund, 1908

PAGE 8: Leslie Jean-Bart; source, Scalamandre Archive, New York

PAGE 13: Oil on panel, courtesy the J. Paul Getty Museum, Malibu, California

PAGES 14 AND 15: Courtesy the J. Paul Getty Museum, Malibu, California

PAGES 18-19: Courtesy the Sadberk Hanim Museum, Istanbul

PAGE 20: Courtesy the J. Paul Getty Museum, Malibu, California

PAGE 24: Courtesy the Smith-Telfer Collection, the New York State Historical Association, Cooperstown

PAGE 29: Source, Scalamandre Archive, New York

PAGE 31: Oil on canvas, courtesy the Metropolitan Museum of Art, New York, Bequest of Stephen C. Clark, 1960

PAGES 34-35: Oil on canvas, courtesy The Frick Collection, New York

PAGE 37: Source, Scalamandre Archive, New York

PAGE 39: Courtesy the Dance Collection, The New York Public Library for the Performing Arts, Astor, Lenox and Tilden Foundations

PAGE 41: Courtesy Oscar de la Renta

PAGE 45: Courtesy the New York Metropolitan Opera

PAGE 51: Courtesy the J. Paul Getty Museum, Malibu, California

PAGE 55: Courtesy Arthur Sanderson and Sons Ltd., New York

PAGE 56: Courtesy Tiffany & Co., New York

PAGE 58: Courtesy Ungaro

PAGE 59: Courtesy the J. Paul Getty Museum, Malibu, California

PAGE 60: Courtesy Philadelphia Museum of Art, Bequest of Charlotte Dorrance Wright

PAGE 64: Courtesy J. Paul Getty Museum, Malibu, California

PAGE 65: Courtesy Christie's, New York

PAGE 67: Courtesy the Private Collection of Mr. and Mrs. Walter H. Annenberg

PAGE 68: Courtesy Sotheby's, New York

PAGE 86: Courtesy Sühendan Kumcu, Istanbul University

PAGE 87: Courtesy the Sadberk Hanim Museum, Istanbul

PAGE 88: Copyright Lance Dane

PAGE 89: Copyright Anil Modi

PAGES 110 TO 121: Source, Scalamandre Archive, New York

PAGES 136 AND 137, ABOVE RIGHT: Permission of *House & Garden*

PAGE 143: Courtesy Rebus, Inc., New York

Acknowledgements

෨

My gratitude to J.-C. Suarès for conceiving the idea for this book and turning it into an object of beauty; to Peter C. Jones for his long, diligent labors; to the Gates Sisters for their precision and professionalism; to Sarah Poole for her loving assistance; to John Anderson for the refinement of his skillful copy editing; and to Peter Warner for his guiding hand and patience. My thanks also to others who contributed their time and knowledge: Leslie Degeorges at Scalamandre; Barbara Pesch at the Brooklyn Botanic Garden; Dr. Nurhan Atasoy and Sühendan Kumcu of Istanbul University; Tim Smith of the W. Graham Arader III Gallery; and all the photographers and artists whose imagery makes this book a celebration.

This book was set in 11, 12 and 14 point Garamond-Stemple.

nominis, et præsta in nobis christian

tum, vt tuo diuino auxilio nutriti,